How To Emotionally Connect

The Ultimate Guide On How To Be Emotionally Available

Stephanie Mike

Table of Contents

Introduction

As humans, we all seek emotional connection. Feeling connected to individuals in our lives provides us with a much-needed sense of affection and belonging, as well as support during life's ups and downs.

Deep attachments have surprise long-term rewards. For starters, strong social ties can have a significant positive impact on our mental health. A study published in 2022 in The International Journal of Public Health discovered that having more social connections can reduce your risk of experiencing anxiety and sadness. Feeling seen and heard by another person can help to alleviate our mental burden. Emotional connection is essential for mental health because it gives a secure area for people to express their true feelings, both positive and negative.

Close relationships with friends, family, or a love partner can also have a positive impact on health. A study that was published in The American Journal of Lifestyle Medicine found that those who have close social ties tend to live longer and have lower rates of diabetes, obesity, and cancer.

Of course, not all relationships result in or are suitable for profound emotional attachment. And, depending on your previous circumstances, you might not know what healthy emotional closeness looks like. Here's how experts describe positive emotional connection, as well as how to nurture it in romantic relationships, platonic friendships, and familial ties.

Scientific equipment are unable to observe or quantify emotional connection, and different people will interpret it in different ways. Nonetheless, some traits stand out. Healthy emotional connections include being yourself, feeling at ease and capable of exposing yourself, offering compassion, receiving equal support, and having fun with the other person.

Our interactions with ourselves have a big impact on the relationships we have with other people. A person's ability to develop emotionally close to someone begins with their ability to be emotionally close to themselves, which, like most other aspects of life and relationships, stems from our early attachment experiences with our primary caregivers. If you are having difficulty connecting emotionally with the people in your life due to a painful past, treatment with a certified therapist may be beneficial.

Finally, in healthy relationships, vulnerability is what brings us closer to another person. Transparency and a strong sense of connection are essential for healthy relationships. When we are not vulnerable in our relationships, we miss out on opportunities to build trust and intimacy via emotional openness.

The ability to express oneself honestly and without judgment enhances connections. If both couples are comfortable being open and honest, they can process their feelings with less shame and more understanding. This mutual sharing allows both sides to build trust. And, according to studies published in Psychological Reports, trust is a strong predictor of relationship health, particularly romantic ones.

Chapter 1

Emotional Connection in Relationship

There it is again. You can feel it between you two. It's the sensation of being drawn further into something sweet and terrifying. You want to follow your feelings, but you're also terrified of what they may disclose. You're not sure if you're the only one wondering if you're feeling a deep emotional connection with the other person. How can you tell anyway? What exactly does it mean to be emotionally intimate with someone, and why is it both alluring and frightening? How do you develop or sustain emotional intimacy in a relationship?

Emotional closeness occurs when we open up to another person on a deep level. It takes a leap of faith and a lot of confidence that our partner will not intentionally hurt us with the details we disclose about ourselves. We all have things we wouldn't like to disclose with others, yet it is a basic human desire to be fully recognized for who we are and loved regardless. This is why we incur the risk of giving information that exposes us to rejection or abuse if our partner fails to honor our trust. Among the topics we might discuss include:

- ❖ *Secrets from our past, such as family trauma, abuse, or things we've done wrong*
- ❖
- ❖ *Our deepest feelings*
- ❖
- ❖ *Fragile hopes and dreams that we believe others would not understand.*
- ❖
- ❖ *Future ambitions that others may tear down or reject.*
- ❖
- ❖ *Our inner universe of imagination.*
- ❖
- ❖ *Our weaknesses and failings*
- ❖
- ❖ *Anything that makes us seem weak or vulnerable.*
- ❖
- ❖ *Secrets we are ashamed of.*

You feel you "get" each other
Feeling understood and appreciated for who you are is an important aspect of any relationship. When you develop an emotional connection with another individual, it is one of the first indications that something deeper is going on. Since you both understand one other, it's a compelling sense that piques your interest in finding out more about the other person.

You're comfortable discussing anything
Have you ever had a best buddy who you could chat to about anything, and nothing was off-limits? Emotional connection in friendship is comparable to what occurs in an emotionally comfortable relationship: you may discuss everything. When you are able to conduct conversations with someone you wouldn't normally talk to, you know you have connected emotionally.

You value the other person's opinions
In a deepening emotional relationship, you regard the other person's opinions on a wide range of topics, particularly contentious ones that you would not often discuss with others. You value ideas and guidance on everyday concerns.

Emotional attraction occurs before physical attraction
Emotional connection often comes before physical attraction in an emotionally intimate setting. You require both for a complete and healthy connection. However, when you are drawn to someone because of their mind or personality, it indicates that your relationship is developing a stronger emotional connection.

You listen to each other
Feeling heard and understood is a vital foundation for emotional intimacy. When you care for someone, you want to hear them talk about what is important to them, which is also important to you because of how much they mean to you. In a healthy and equal partnership, they will reciprocate.

You know you can trust one another

Trust is a fundamental component of emotional closeness. You can tell you have a strong emotional bond when you know you can share your innermost secrets with one other and that you will stand by each other no matter what.

You respect each other

No relationship is without strife at all times. There will be instances when you disagree. In a relationship characterized by a strong emotional bond, respect for one another always underlies disagreements and disputes. On the surface, you still love each other and believe in all of the reasons you came together in the first place. You understand that disputes are not the end of the relationship and that you will heal the damage while continuing to love each other. This is indicative of a mature relationship with a high degree of emotional intimacy.

Your Emotional Connection To a Man

Women tend to be more emotionally open than men because they are better at perceiving and processing feelings. Men tend to use rationality first, which can be perplexing for a woman who is unsure how he feels or where she stands with him. Having said that, a mentally well man who is prepared for a partnership looks for emotional kinship. It might take him a little longer to figure out what he wants. Signs that you are developing an emotional connection with him:

He is caring and typically prioritizes your happiness

In any healthy relationship, the partners consider one other's pleasure and typically prioritize the other person's interests over their own. If your partner does something for you, it shows that he cares about you.

Silence is comforting

When you can enjoy quiet together without feeling the need to chat to fill the gap, it indicates that you are emotionally comfortable with each other. If one of you is uncomfortable with quiet, it could indicate that your emotional connection remains superficial.

He respects you

Respect is crucial to a man, and how he respects you reveals a lot about his feelings for you. Respect means that he will avoid doing or saying anything that will harm or embarrass you.

He communicates with you when things go awry

When he tells you about his difficulties or wants to vent after a rough day, it shows that he respects and trusts your perspective. He could probably talk to other individuals, but he chose you because of the emotional bond you two have.

He wants to spend time with you

If you always seem to be waiting for your boyfriend to make time for you, it means you don't have a strong emotional connection. When a man is emotionally attracted to you, he enjoys spending time with you and looks forward to your interactions. He also enjoys hearing you discuss topics that are important to you.

Small nuances are significant to him

When he remembers small information about you, you know you have an emotional connection. It suggests they are as important to him as you are. They are likely to be items that others might not remember or consider essential, such as your favorite color, flower, or meal.

Your Emotional Connection To a Woman

If you've met an attractive woman and want to further your relationship, how do you know if there's a genuine emotional connection? Navigating the intricate world of a woman's emotions

can be difficult for men, but here are some indicators that you're on
the right track:

You actively listen to one another

Communication is essential in any good relationship, but it is
especially necessary for most women. Active listening implies that
she is there while you are speaking, and vice versa. With the goal of
comprehending one another, you listen to one another. Rephrasing
each other's words helps you understand the meaning. You keep
eye contact while speaking and do not allow distractions like your
phone to disrupt the conversation. Genuine discourse is a
fundamental component of emotional connection.

She is real with you

Nothing creates an emotional connection like sincerity. When a lady
is her true self around you, it indicates that she is at ease with you
and does not feel the need to hide, play games, or put up a fake
front. She is natural and sincere, and honesty will thrive in the
partnership.

You can be yourself with her

Have you ever felt that you couldn't be yourself around a lady
because she might react negatively? That is a clear indication that
you are not comfortable enough with her to form a genuine emotional
relationship. However, finding someone with whom you can be
absolutely honest is gold. When you can be yourself and she just
laughs it off and accepts you, you're making a true connection.

She is affectionate

Most women enjoy receiving non-sexual affection, such as a hug
from the back, a kiss on the neck, or a back rub. So if your girlfriend
is doing these things for you, it means she is happy and safe in the
relationship and feels comfortable expressing your attention.
Returning her affection will enhance your emotional bond.

She does small things that she knows you enjoy

When a lady feels genuine about you, she will do small things for you
that she knows you enjoy. Pay attention, because this indicates that

your relationship is important to her. And when you do the same for her, she will be grateful that you notice the little things about her. The little things improve your emotional bond. Men often believe that they must go to great lengths to impress a lady, yet a genuine woman values small gestures just as much as large ones.

She gives you compliments
When a woman feels a stronger connection with you, she will frequently show appreciation or respect for you. Listen to her talk with others: Does she make good remarks about you? If she does, you can be confident that she is emotionally drawn to you. Make sure you reciprocate her pleasant phrases.

She wants to be there for you
Life does not always run smoothly. Health troubles, career problems, and other issues can all have a negative impact on relationships. But if you're going through a difficult moment and your girlfriend wants to be there for you, it means she's emotionally invested in you and the relationship.

She wants to spend time with you
Building an emotional connection requires time. What is quality time? That looks different for each couple, but it is engaging in things that are meaningful to both of them or spending time together that fosters emotional intimacy. Quality time does not involve developing habits or rituals, such as spending all of your free time together in front of the television. When you do this, you are together but not engaging in meaningful activities that strengthen your relationship.

She cares for your family
A genuine woman will care about the things that are important to you. If that is your family, she will treat them with civility, care, and respect because they are a significant part of your life.

Bad Habits Can Be Lethal To Emotional Closeness

When a couple has been married for a while, it's easy to let routine, boredom, or bad behaviors cause emotional distance. Inadequate communication, repressed emotions, a partner who is emotionally unavailable, mistrust, and secrets are all signs that an emotionally distant marriage is developing. Take into account the following advice if you feel that your relationship lacks emotional connection:

Make time for each other on purpose.

Set restrictions for your time together, such as no phones.

Work on becoming a safe presence in your spouse's life. This includes fighting fairly, avoiding harsh behavior such as name-calling, and deciding not to purposely do something that would harm your partner.

Do small things you know your partner likes. Send him a text expressing your admiration or attraction. Get up early and make her favorite brew when she wakes up. These Simple things help to strengthen emotional connection in a relationship.

Do something to spark conversation. For example, read a book together and then debate it. Alternatively, set aside a regular period free of interruptions to discuss what's going on in each other's lives.

Maintain a balance between connection and individuality. Too much of either is unhealthy. To be healthy together, you must both function as independent, entire persons. Maintaining a successful relationship requires striking the appropriate balance between spending too much and not enough time together.

Join a marriage enrichment event. Many couples believe that these occasions help them keep the spark in their relationships.

Make a list of activities you enjoy or want to do, and then plan to do them together.

If your relationship is in serious turmoil, you might consider obtaining help. This could imply that one of you goes to counseling if the other does not want to; you cannot force a reluctant spouse to go. This will cause more harm than good. However, counseling can be beneficial even if just one person attends because it can help you cope with emotional stress or distance. It can also assist you in changing direction if you have habits that are damaging your relationship.

Making An Emotional Connection Before Getting Physical

Many women require an emotional connection with their partner in order to enjoy sex. If your girlfriend isn't as excited about a night between the sheets as you are, attempt to connect with her emotionally first.

Good communication is frequently the beginning of an emotional relationship for women

Be present and attentive while she speaks; do not allow distractions to come between the two of you. Ask her about her day or get her opinion on something. Show her that you value your interactions with her just as much as you do.

Pay attention to her attempts to connect

Partners frequently try emotional connection, only for the other person to misinterpret it. Keep an eye out for questions that appear to be bothersome or intrusive. Be careful not to disregard it because she may be trying to connect with you. Is she making a flirty joke or doing anything she knows will catch your attention? By observing these subtle indicators, you can increase her emotional attachment to you and her likelihood of wanting sex.

Enter her world

When you can see things from your partner's perspective, you develop empathy and connection. Hugs, kind or tender words, or doing small things for her that she enjoys are all ways to show her that you care about what she is experiencing. Avoid the desire to give counsel or fix problems; doing so promotes detachment, even if it appears to be the reasonable thing for a man to do. By listening and loving, you enable her to solve the situation on her own, even if it takes a long time.

Open up to yourself

Good communication is more than just listening; it also entails opening yourself and being vulnerable. Trust and connection are formed when both people divulge more about themselves, trusting that the other person will handle that information with care and respect.

Let her know you have her back

A lady needs to know that she is more important to you than anyone or anything else. Let her know that your loyalty is with her and that she is your top priority. She will feel comfortable trusting you, which will increase your emotional bond. However, don't just say it once; find methods to show her how valuable she is to you and that you are there for her.

When a strong emotional connection is established, most couples will experience better sex and a more fulfilling love life. For men, sex is frequently the start of an emotional connection, whereas, for many women, the emotional connection must come first before they feel sexually responsive. Couples who understand this dynamic and strike the correct balance are more likely to have successful relationships.

Chapter 2

Building Empathy

Knowing, being aware of, being receptive to, and vicariously experiencing another's feelings, thoughts, and experiences in the past or present without the feelings, thoughts, and experiences being fully stated objectively.

Empathy is one of the most fundamental parts of developing great connections, lowering stress, and increasing emotional awareness, yet it can be challenging at times. For example, how can you be empathic to someone with whom you disagree?

I believe myself to be an empathic person, but I've noticed that with some people and situations, my natural capacity and desire to empathize is diminished or non-existent especially these days.

However, the majority of people are ignorant of the many advantages of empathy. For example, I've seen that when I feel empathy for others and myself, I have a sense of tranquility, connection, and perspective that I enjoy. And, when there is a lack of empathy in a relationship, circumstance, or in how I relate to myself, I frequently experience stress, detachment, and negative emotions. Can you relate?

Empathy is not the same as sympathy. When we are empathetic, we often pity others while keeping a physical, mental, and emotional distance from their feelings or experiences. More accurately, empathy is the feeling that we can completely understand, connect to, or visualize the depth of the emotional state or situation of another person.

It means that you feel with someone rather than sorry for them. The English word empathy is derived from the German word einfühlung, which means "to feel as one with." It entails sharing the load or putting yourself in the shoes of another person to comprehend their point of view.

The Benefits of Empathy

Another reason empathy is so important is that it is one of the most effective methods to improve our relationships, reduce stress, and feel good about ourselves and our lives in an authentic manner. Here are some other major benefits of empathy:

- *Less stress and negativity lead to better health and stronger immune systems.*
- *Leads to a happy life.*
- *Improves communication skills.*
- *Leads to collaboration.*
- *Promotes a healthy work environment.*
- *Transcends personal ties.*
- *Reduces negativity.*

Why People Lack Empathy

A variety of factors impede our ability to use and experience the power of empathy. Three of the major ones, all interconnected, are as follows:

Feeling threatened
We frequently feel "threatened" because of our own anxieties, projections, and past experiences, rather than what is actually happening in the moment or in a specific relationship or scenario. When we feel threatened in any way, whether it is "actual" or "imagined," our ability to perceive empathy is frequently shut off.

Being Judgmental

Being judgmental is not the same as making value judgments about what to dress, eat, or say.

When we are judgmental, we decide that we are "right" and others are "wrong." This causes harm to ourselves and others, as well as isolation from those around us. When we make judgments about another person, group of people, or situation, we drastically reduce our ability to empathize.

Fear

Fear is not necessarily wrong; it is a natural human feeling with many positive features if we are prepared to admit, own, express, and move through it. Fear preserves our lives and keeps us out of peril at all times.

Fear is a problem because we deny its existence. We label things, people, or situations as "frightening," yet there is nothing in life that is intrinsically "scary. It becomes challenging, if not impossible, to harness the power of empathy when we allow ourselves to be driven by fear. This frequently results in us defending ourselves against "threats," passing judgment on others, and other behaviors.

I frequently discuss the significance of embracing our emotions. Our capacity for empathy increases with the degree to which we are prepared to face, name, accept, and own our fear.

Signs that someone lacks empathy

Here are several indicators that someone lacks empathy.

- ❖ *Very judgmental of others.*
- ❖
- ❖ *Unable to regulate emotions.*
- ❖
- ❖ *Unaware of other people's sentiments.*
- ❖
- ❖ *Accuses individuals of being excessively sensitive.*

- ❖
- ❖ *Overreacts to tiny things.*
- ❖
- ❖ *Will not admit when incorrect.*
- ❖
- ❖ *Behaves insensitively.*
- ❖
- ❖ *Has difficulty maintaining relationships.*
- ❖
- ❖ *Cannot handle uncomfortable situations.*
- ❖
- ❖ *Observe perceived slights everywhere.*

Empathy is crucial because it allows us to better understand how others are experiencing and even experience it ourselves. It helps us sustain relationships and influences our performance in both personal and professional relationships. A lack of empathy is also a feature of personality disorders such as narcissism and antisocial personality disorder.

People may lack empathy because of the circumstances in which they were reared. They may have grown up with parents who were unable to control their emotions and showed no compassion for them. They may have also been through traumatic experiences in their lives, which has led to a lack of empathy and the behavior they exhibit.

How to Be More Empathetic

Be honest about how you feel

When we are in a conflict with another person or dealing with someone or something that is difficult for us, being able to acknowledge, own, and convey our fear, insecurity, sadness, rage, jealousy, or whatever other negative emotions we are experiencing is one of the most effective ways for us to move past our evasion and genuinely address the deeper issues of the situation.

This permits us to develop empathy for ourselves, the other individuals involved, and even the circumstances surrounding the conflict or issue.

Imagine what it is like for them
While it can be difficult to "understand" another person's perspective or circumstance, being able to envision what it must be like for them is an important part of empathy.

The more willing we are to envision what life is like for them, the more understanding, sympathy, and empathy we will be able to feel. In today's unstable political atmosphere and the numerous difficulties associated with a pandemic, it is more necessary than ever to practice compassion on a daily basis.

Forgiveness is one of many crucial components of life, although it is frequently easier said than done. It is something we should always learn about and practice.

Chapter 3

Communication skills

I've noticed that attentive listening is the foundation of good communication in relationships, whether at business, with friends, or in personal relationships. It is the willingness to fully hear and understand the opinions, emotions, and experiences of others we care about. Active listening has allowed me to create a space for honest and meaningful talks, establishing the framework for deeper interactions based on mutual respect and empathy.

Equally important in the field of good communication is the discipline of assertiveness combined with empathy. It is the ability to express one's thoughts, feelings, and needs clearly and respectfully, while also being aware of other people's emotions and viewpoints. I've discovered that practicing assertive communication has allowed me to honor my authenticity while also cultivating an environment of mutual understanding and respect in my relationships.

The road to learning successful communication has revealed the importance of nonverbal clues and body language. It's the subtle yet powerful way we communicate empathy, validation, and support to individuals we engage with. By developing an understanding of nonverbal communication, I've enhanced the emotional resonance of my encounters, building a sense of trust and connection that goes beyond words.

Furthermore, I've found that practicing excellent communication has helped me navigate disagreements and resolve differences in my relationships. By creating an environment that encourages open communication, I've discovered that disputes become chances for growth, understanding, and the strengthening of my bonds with people. Through effective communication, I've learned to approach issues with empathy and a real desire for resolution, establishing trust and harmony in my relationships.

There were periods of confusion, misunderstandings, and difficulty in finding the appropriate words. However, with time, self-reflection, and a dedication to progress, I've realized that effective communication is a talent that can be developed and perfected, thereby enriching the fabric of my relationships.

As we move forward, this will most likely not be the last time I discuss it, so keep in mind that successful communication is a dynamic and continuing practice that fosters trust, understanding, and intimacy within the fabric of our connections.

Words are the most powerful tool we have, both individually and collectively, as humans. The ability to communicate is a crucial component of being alive. With words, we have been able to express ourselves in artwork, literature, and music, elevating our civilizations and cultures around the world. Our verbal and creative expressions are essential to our humanity.

The question is, do we communicate properly with one another? We communicate and convey our ideas and convictions through writing and voice, but do we actively listen to each other? Active listening is a critical component of our individual success, whether in our personal interactions with loved ones, families, and friends or in our workplace and corporate partnerships. Our ability to slow down and create room inside ourselves to pay attention and truly listen to one another is critical, and it will decide how far we move. Our ability to listen with focus and intent will determine how successful we are throughout our lives.

The biggest issue with modern communication is that we don't listen to comprehend. We listen to responses. This turns out to be a surefire technique to spark tension and misconceptions, complicating a conversation. When we chat and establish a conversation, the speaker's purpose should be to actively listen and understand the meaning of the words stated. When we speak, we are only affirming what was previously understood.

When we listen, we gain knowledge and diverse points of view, which become part of our wisdom. For example, you and a loved one may have personal misunderstandings at times. Trust me, it occurs to everyone on a regular basis. Simple misunderstandings can escalate into massive fights. Have you ever tried to simply listen without complaining or arguing your point of view?

Do you put yourself in someone else's shoes? Listening has the ability to de-escalate any potentially volatile scenario. It can work wonders if you are fully engaged and strive to comprehend your loved one's point of view. Listening entails lowering the ego and accepting the reality that you are not perfect and that even the best among us make errors. If you can acquire this level of insight and genuine empathy for your loved ones, your relationships will improve.

The best personal and business partnerships are those in which both partners listen to each other and come to an agreement or compromise. No relationship is easy or perfect, but being able to listen and comprehend each other's points of view goes a long way toward building a strong foundation of mutual respect, love, trust, and friendship. Listen to each other with interest and understanding, speak honestly, and behave with integrity and morality. Choose this as your mantra and work toward enlightenment by paying close attention to your many contacts and interactions in your life.

Communication is an art, and we must work diligently to grow and achieve a level of skill and quality. It is definitely not easy and requires years of practice and patience to master. Listening is as vital if not more than speaking.

Effective Methods to Make Others Feel Important

- ❖ *Use their name.*
- ❖
- ❖ *Express heartfelt gratitude.*
- ❖
- ❖ *Do more listening than speaking.*
- ❖

❖ *Talk more about them than about yourself.*

❖ *Be genuinely interested.*

❖ *Be sincere in your praise.*

❖ *Show that you care.*

The elements of effective communication are actively listening, being present, demonstrating empathy, and mindfulness, bridging whatever gaps we may have with others, and engaging in open discourse. These are the methods for fostering understanding and harmony in our interactions with others. We are all complex beings with complex emotions, but as long as people exhibit compassion and a willingness to appreciate someone else's point of view, they will become more open and vibrant. Words are powerful, but listening requires mastery.

Chapter 4

Emotional Support

Providing emotional support often entails asking questions, listening, and then providing affirmation and the form of support a person requires, whether physical closeness or something else.

You could help a loved one in need financially as well as physically by supporting someone who is having trouble standing or walking. Other types of support are also crucial. Individuals in your life who offer social and emotional support, such family, friends, and even close colleagues, might make you feel better.

People provide emotional support to others by expressing real encouragement, reassurance, and compassion. This could include verbal statements of sympathy or physical displays of affection. Other kinds of emotional support include religion or spirituality, community activities, and even your pets. Whatever form it takes, this assistance can improve anyone's outlook and overall well-being.

Some people are inherently good at being emotionally helpful, but this is not the case for everyone. However, with some effort, you may improve these skills.

When you want to provide emotional support to a person you care about, ask a few questions beforehand. "How can I help you?" is occasionally effective, but it is not always the right strategy. While these queries are motivated by good intentions, they may not always have the desired impact. People do not always know what they want or need, especially when faced with a challenging situation. So, this question can be so wide that someone is unclear on how to respond.

Instead, consider asking questions adapted to a scenario or the person's state of mind, such as:

You appear upset today. Would you like to discuss it?

I understand your boss was treating you poorly. How are you holding up?

If you know someone who has had some hardships and is unsure how to start a conversation, consider starting with some general questions, such as, "What's been happening in your life lately?"

Keep your queries open-ended rather than asking questions that may be answered with a "yes" or a "no." This prompts an explanation and keeps the topic going.

It's not enough to just ask questions. Another key aspect of offering emotional support is active listening, often known as empathy. When you truly listen to someone, you offer them your complete attention. Demonstrate attention in their remarks by:

Using open body language, such as turning toward them, relaxing your face, or keeping your arms and legs uncrossed.

Avoid distractions, such as fiddling with your cell phone or thinking about other things you need to do.

Instead of interrupting, nod in agreement with their words.

Seek explanation if something isn't clear.

Summarizing what they've stated to demonstrate you have a thorough understanding of the scenario

Using effective listening skills demonstrates that you care about what others are going through. Knowing that someone else has heard their anguish can be quite beneficial to someone who is struggling.

When was the last time you encountered a difficult circumstance? You probably wanted to talk to someone about the situation, but you didn't necessarily want them to solve it or make it go away. Perhaps you simply wanted to express your frustration or disappointment and receive some calming recognition in return.

Support does not require you to fully comprehend a problem or offer a solution. Often, it is simply validation. When you validate someone, you are letting them know that you recognize and understand their viewpoint.

Recognition of one's pain is typically the most desired form of help. So, when a loved one informs you about the difficulties they're facing, they may not require your assistance. You may be able to provide the best help simply by expressing concern and being there.

Nobody enjoys feeling judged. Someone confronting a bad circumstance as a result of their actions may have already engaged in self-judgment. Regardless, when individuals seek help, they do not want to hear criticism, even if it is offered constructively and with the best of intentions.

When offering support, try not to share your thoughts on what they should have done or where they went wrong. Avoid asking inquiries that they might see as accusing or judging, such as, "So what got them so furious at you?

Even if you don't provide direct judgment or criticism, tone can transmit a lot of emotion, so your voice may express emotions you didn't intend to utter out loud. To avoid coming across as condemning, concentrate on emotions like sympathy and compassion while you communicate.

You might think you're assisting someone by advising them how to fix a problem. But generally speaking, people wait to seek legal advice until they particularly desire it. Even if you feel you have the best option, don't provide it unless they expressly ask, "What do you think I should do?" or "Are there any resources that you could recommend?"

If they've progressed beyond "venting" to "talking through the problem," a better technique frequently entails asking introspective questions to help them identify their own answers.

When you want to help someone, don't worry too much about whether you're giving them the "right" kind of assistance. Two separate people are unlikely to offer support in the same way. That's fine, though, because there are many ways to help someone.

Your approach may also vary depending on the person you want to help. Instead of looking for the perfect words to say, go with what seems natural and authentic. An honest display of worry is likely to mean considerably more to your loved one than a prefabricated reaction or one that lacks genuine emotion.

Personal difficulties, particularly those involving rejection, can depress people and cause them to doubt themselves and their talents. If you see someone you care about feeling down, being harsher on themselves than usual, or experiencing self-doubt, a genuine compliment can go a long way toward improving their mood.

When giving compliments, keep the following points in mind
Keep them relevant to the present circumstance. For example, you could tell a friend who is unhappy about a mistake at work about their typical pattern of success.

Choose remarks that emphasize individual strengths versus generic compliments that may apply to anyone. Instead of simply saying "You're very considerate," identify what makes them thoughtful and express your admiration for that quality.

Do not gush. A well-placed compliment can make someone feel good. Excessive compliments might make people skeptical or even uncomfortable, even if you truly mean them.

When a close friend or love partner believes they have found a solution to their problem, you may have reservations about its usefulness. Unless their approach includes some risk or danger, it is often preferable to give assistance rather than point out flaws in their strategy.

They may not have taken the same strategy as you, but that does not make them incorrect. Even if you don't see their solution working, you can't predict how things will turn out for certain. Avoid telling them what you think they should do, as this can sometimes ruin the great sensations that you've already provided.

If they ask what you think, you may give them some polite advice that will assist their idea succeed. Even if they ask for your honest opinion, don't answer with harsh or negative comments, or tear apart their strategy.

Physical affection is not suitable in all circumstances
Hugs, kisses, and other intimate touches and caresses can frequently have a profound impact on the person you wish to assist.

After a stressful conversation, hugging someone can provide physical comfort while also reinforcing the emotional support you just provided.

Holding a loved one's hand as they undergo a difficult operation, receive bad news, or deal with a traumatic phone call might make them feel stronger. Cuddling with your lover after a rough day can convey your feelings for them and provide healing comfort.

People confront a variety of unpleasant situations in life. Some of these difficulties have far broader or far-reaching implications than others. It is not for anybody else to decide how upset someone should, or should not be over a particular form of discomfort.

Comparing a loved one's challenges to those of others is often done accidentally as a kind of consolation. You may try to cheer them up by saying things like, "It could be a lot more severe," or "At least you still have a job. This contradicts their experience and frequently implies that they shouldn't feel bad in the first place. Never discount someone's concern, regardless of how insignificant it may seem to you.

Yes, you might not have been offended by the lecture your best friend's boss gave her. However, you cannot fully comprehend her experience or emotional response, thus it is not fair to minimize her sentiments.

Certain challenging problems have no answer. You can listen to your loved one's anguish and provide physical and emotional assistance. However, when time is the sole solution to their condition, you may both feel helpless.

You can still offer assistance, however. Someone in a difficult situation may struggle to focus on other things. They may wish to distract themselves from tension and concern but don't know where to start. You, on the other hand, are probably far enough removed from the situation to generate a few ideas to divert their attention away from their problems.

Aim for an enjoyable, low-key activity that can be rescheduled if they don't feel up to it. You can't go wrong with anything you know they'll appreciate, such as a walk down a favorite nature route or a visit to the dog park. If you can't go outside, consider a craft, home project, or game instead.

Emotional support is intangible. You can't see it or hold it, and its impact may not be immediately apparent, especially if you're struggling. But it might serve as a reminder that others love, value, and support you.

When you provide emotional support to others, you are letting them know they are not alone. This message may have a greater long-term positive influence on mental health than brief mood boosters or forms of assistance.

Chapter 5

Emotional Connections In The Workplace

Use emotion to inspire and motivate others to perform at their best. When I talk about emotional connection with executives, I don't mean excessive displays of emotion, oversharing of personally identifiable data, or engaging in therapy sessions with colleagues. It's about engaging with our colleagues, coworkers, and bosses as emotional humans rather than task-focused automatons. The feelings that you, as a leader, elicit in others allow you to bring out the best in them.

Aristotle recognized pathos as an important aspect of communication and persuasion thousands of years ago. Pathos, in philosophy and rhetoric, is a deliberate appeal to emotion in order to elicit specific feelings in the listener. Aristotle realized long ago that the human connection is extremely important in eliciting action. As the maxim goes, reasoning makes us think, but emotions make us act.

Here are three ways I've advised leaders to use emotion to encourage their teams and achieve greater outcomes:

Cultivate the energy that comes from enthusiasm
Most of us have experienced increased wind in our sails when we are enthusiastic about a project or the work we undertake. As a leader, you may harness this energy by sharing your enthusiasm for the goals that must be reached. However, you may have to gain access to it first.

I worked with a chief data officer who was unquestionably the most knowledgeable person in the company when it came to analytics. I wouldn't call him negative, but he definitely lacked a positive spark. He realized the importance of getting out of the spreadsheets and using data to engage with others, both about the issues they were passionate about fixing and the business results they were looking forward to achieving. I proposed that he focus on three questions:

* *What about this topic makes me optimistic?*
* *How does it relate to a larger conclusion than we are discussing?*
* *How can I convey this with positive energy?*

After six months of constant efforts to boost productivity, his peers, direct reports, and the CEO saw that he was a stronger collaborator with a broader perspective on the business. They found him more calculative and motivating.

This is not meant to imply a false positive. It's most effective to regularly connect your team's everyday work to your long-term vision: a necessary set of tasks or a short-term grind can result in significant consequences for your customers, patients, visitors, the business, or the environment. Whatever the outcome, having a clear line of sight with vigor can provide a strong drive forward.

Recognize the source of your anger and channel it more effectively
Anger has its place in leadership. It is a powerful feeling that motivates action, offering important energy when articulating concerns and fears and communicating urgency. Unfortunately, rage is frequently misdirected and loses its potency.

Expressing anger through yelling or raising your voice, cutting others off, or speaking aggressively is likely to result in strong defensiveness or shutting down from others. For leaders, the most effective method to communicate rage is to rationally express the underlying worry. In business, fury is usually the manifestation of fear or concern about what will happen if something does not go as planned. Alternatively, it could be protecting against worry and distress about the implications of a terrible outcome. Frequently, the feelings that drive rage can help you connect more meaningfully and strengthen relationships.

The next time you're upset, take a deep breath and question yourself:

* *Am I angry, or am I experiencing something else?*
*
* *If you respond, "I'm just mad!," consider a few alternative choices. Afraid? Distressed? Worried? What is this about?*
*
* *How can I explain myself in a collected manner that inspires positive action?*

This level of honesty about your emotions is known as vulnerability, and it may be a catalyst for establishing trust, collaboration, and teamwork. However, for those who are not fully comfortable with this term, simply focus on using your anger more productively. Try lowering the heat and calmly expressing unhappiness with a situation, addressing your concerns, and openly encouraging others to voice their thoughts. This allows for frank discussions with team members about not achieving a standard or expectation, which can ultimately motivate your team to put in more effort, correct key errors, and finally address long-standing issues.

Encourage deeper participation by focusing on development
Coaching and developing others is one of the most powerful tools a leader can use to inspire people to perform at their best. When people tell me about the best leaders they've worked under, they almost always mention how interested those leaders were in their professional development.

Mentoring and coaching foster emotional bonds that benefit both parties in the long run. Leaders that place a high priority on their team members' development attest that it gives them a sense of strength, importance, and power. They take great pride in imparting their knowledge and seeing their staff members advance and prosper. Those who have been coached believe that the confidence a leader demonstrated in them by spending time and resources in their development helped them feel more interested in their work, raised their own confidence, and, as a result, improved their performance.

Communicate your dedication and build a shared vision of achievement by saying the following to individuals you coach:

- ❖ *Your professional development is vital to me and our staff.*
- ❖
- ❖ *I have faith in your potential and skills.*
- ❖
- ❖ *I'm willing to provide the time and resources required to assist you achieve your objectives.*

Focusing on employee development is an investment that will yield long-term company advantages. Time spent assisting people in improving their performance fuels the emotional connection that leads to employee loyalty, motivation, and increased team success. A boss who mentored me once said, "My commitment to your development isn't wholly altruistic. I am confident that the more you improve, the better our outcomes will be.

It's easy to get caught up in the whirlwind of all that has to be done and lose sight of our primary duty as leaders, which is to drive results via others. Including emotion in your toolkit of leadership skills does not need a lot of additional work. It does take a willingness to engage differently. Be willing to explain how you are feeling in order to connect with people and understand how they are experiencing as well. In my experience, the more leaders focus on this, the better the outcomes for those they lead.

Chapter 6

Emotional Connections In The Digital Age

They stated, "Quality over quantity". What then is the true relationship to which I am alluding? An honest and meaningful bond created between people via shared experiences, mutual understanding, and trust is known as a genuine connection. It extends beyond surface interactions to include a sense of vulnerability and emotional connection.

In today's fast-paced, technology-driven society, it's easy to fall into the trap of superficial connections, such as social media friendships or chance encounters. While these connections can bring a sense of belonging and convenience, they frequently lack depth and genuine emotional connection.

I recently found myself in a similar predicament, caught in shallow and inauthentic friendships. Instead of bringing consolation, these experiences increased my worry and left me feeling guilty. This is my tale of realizing the dangers of shallow relationships and my quest to make authentic ones.

At first, these shallow alliances were desirable. They provided a sense of belonging and convenience, distracting people from their feelings of loneliness. However, as time went on, I realized that the brief exchanges and surface-level chats left me wanting deeper ties. Despite my frequent social interactions, I felt increasingly lonely and disconnected from my genuine self.

The need to fit in and keep up appearances bore heavily on me. I often wondered if I was being true to myself or merely following the crowd. The guilt I felt afterward was a clear indication that these friendships did not reflect my beliefs and desire for true connections.

My recent experience of being imprisoned in superficial friendships has taught me crucial lessons about the value of building true relationships. Through introspection and self-discovery, I've uncovered essential takeaways to help us develop true connections rather than superficial ones. Here, I share these insights in the hopes of motivating others to make significant connections in their own life.

Embrace vulnerability

To form meaningful friendships, we must embrace vulnerability. It takes guts to open up, disclose our actual selves, and express our thoughts and emotions openly. By letting our guard down, we make room for others to do the same. Vulnerability promotes trust and strengthens bonds, allowing true connections to flourish.

Practice Active Listening

Superficial interactions frequently feature surface-level conversations that lack depth and meaningful engagement. To develop true connections, we must practice active listening. Listening attentively, empathetically, and without judgment enables us to truly comprehend and connect with others. By genuinely interested in their stories, experiences, and viewpoints, we affirm their feelings and make them feel seen and heard.

Cultivate authenticity

Authenticity is the foundation of meaningful relationships. It entails being real to oneself and others, without pretense or masks. When we present ourselves truthfully, we attract like-minded people who value us for who we really are. By embracing our own talents and faults, we create an environment that encourages others to do the same, resulting in meaningful partnerships based on mutual acceptance and understanding.

Foster shared experiences

Shared experiences frequently foster meaningful bonds. Participating in activities or pursuing shared interests allows us to bond and make memorable memories. By participating in shared experiences, we lay the groundwork for meaningful connections to emerge as we overcome challenges, celebrate accomplishments, and support one another along the way.

Invest time and effort

Building true connections takes time and effort. It is not an overnight procedure, but rather an ongoing journey of cultivating and developing relationships. Regular communication, quality time together, and being there for one another during life's ups and downs demonstrate our dedication to developing true connections. This investment of time and effort allows us to create deeper and more rewarding connections.

I learned the value of genuine connections from my recent experience with flimsy friendships. By embracing vulnerability, engaging in active listening, developing authenticity, generating shared experiences, and investing time and energy into fostering meaningful connections, we can improve our quality of life. Let us prioritize quality over quantity, understanding that true fulfillment is found in the depth and sincerity of our relationships with others.

Conclusion

Everyone wants to feel close to the people they care about. However, in order to foster a sense of closeness and intimacy, an emotional connection must be established, whether intentionally or unconsciously.

An emotional connection connects people together and is essential for happy and meaningful partnerships. It's a bond that can make friendships last a lifetime, relationships thrive, and families keep together through good times and bad.

Emotional connection isn't a luxury; it's required for forming healthy, rewarding relationships and maintaining them meaningful and supportive. Building strong emotional bonds with people we admire, our loved ones and our close friends is an investment that pays off in fulfilling relationships.

Recognizing the indicators of a deep emotional connection in your relationships can be reassuring, but don't be concerned if you haven't experienced them all. It is not about checking off all of the boxes on a checklist, but rather about comprehending the multiple dimensions of emotional connections. So, what is the essence of emotional connection? How can you form emotional connections and nurture them in your relationships?

An emotional connection is a unique bond that we share with people we know or admire. It's more than simply discussing the weather or what you ate for lunch. An emotional connection is expressing feelings, being vulnerable, attempting to understand one another, and approaching one another with trust.

Having an emotional connection is more than just chatting; it is about feeling close, respected, and cared for by the other person. It's that warm sensation you get when you know someone is there for you, sincerely listening and trying to comprehend your feelings. Being emotionally attached to someone means being there for them in both good and bad times. This connection strengthens and deepens a relationship by increasing trust.

A strong emotional connection with others is good for your mental health and well-being. It gives people a sense of belonging, security, and support, all of which are necessary for healthy mental health. Understanding emotional connections allows you to go beyond the surface and form meaningful bonds with others.

Signs of Emotional Connection

Emotional connection is modest, yet its existence (or absence) has a substantial impact on the quality of relationships. Here are six signals that you have an emotional connection with someone:

Genuine smiles

When smiles come easily and are genuine, it indicates a positive emotional connection. A genuine smile, one that lights up the eyes, frequently reflects a feeling of joy and understanding shared by two or more people.

Shared laughs

Laughter is the global language of bonding. Shared laughter over inside jokes or comparable experiences typically indicates a stronger emotional link.

A feeling of trust

Trust is essential in any genuine relationship. It's often the first indication of a strong emotional bond. When trust is created, people feel comfortable opening up, embracing vulnerability, and sharing their true selves.

Comfort in silence

Sometimes there is no need for words. Sitting in comfortable quiet, without the desire to fill every minute with superfluous talking or distractions, demonstrates a profound level of understanding between two individuals.

Open communication

Communication is the foundation of any relationship. Open and honest communication frequently indicates a strong emotional connection. It demonstrates a mutual understanding and comfort with expressing yourself.

Nonverbal cues

The capacity to recognize and respond to each other's nonverbal clues, such as gestures, facial expressions, and body language, frequently implies a deeper level of emotional connection.

Reasons Emotional Connection Is Vital In Relationships

Emotional connection transcends the surface and reaches the heart of real human interaction. Attraction draws you to someone. Emotional connection strengthens and holds relationships together.

It can promote greater intimacy in partnerships

Emotional connection is the basis for emotional intimacy. When people connect emotionally, they are more willing to reveal their deepest thoughts, worries, and aspirations, which fosters a stronger bond.

It can build trust

Trust grows when there is an emotional connection. The ability to discuss and comprehend each other's feelings fosters a safe environment in which trust can develop.

It can foster a lifelong bond

A strong emotional attachment can help prevent disagreements, anxiety, and misunderstandings, boosting the likelihood of a long-term partnership.

It improves communication

Emotional connection fosters a conducive climate for open communication. When you feel emotionally linked, you're more likely to communicate successfully and settle issues in a healthy way.

It promotes mental health

Emotional connection provides a sense of belonging and understanding, which can have a substantial impact on your mental health. It offers a vital support system during difficult times.

It promotes self-awareness

Emotionally connected relationships inspire you to think about and comprehend your emotions more deeply.

It promotes life fulfillment

Strong emotional relationships promote general pleasure, life satisfaction, and well-being. They provide depth and purpose to relationships, improving your life experience.

How To Develop Emotional Ties In Relationships

Making an emotional connection does not happen overnight. It necessitates patience, understanding, and transparency. However, there are tangible tactics for cultivating and strengthening emotional connections in your relationships that you can begin today.

Practice active listening

When someone speaks, pause and truly listen. This entails not only hearing what they're saying but also comprehending the feelings underneath them. If you're speaking with someone in person, put down your phone. Make eye contact if possible. Repeat what they say to ensure you grasp it correctly. This demonstrates to the individual that their voice is valuable.

Work toward open communication

Make a comfortable environment for open and honest communication by expressing your thoughts and feelings openly and embracing what the other person has to say without judgment. If something bothers you or makes you happy, share it. This allows both of you to better understand and support one another.

Practice empathy

The capacity to sense and comprehend the emotions of another person is known as empathy. If a friend is sad, attempt to understand their anguish. If they are happy, join in their celebration. Being there for someone emotionally is an excellent technique to establish and strengthen an emotional connection.

Embrace vulnerability

It is acceptable to be completely honest with individuals you trust, including all of your strengths and weaknesses. When you share your concerns or dreams, it encourages the other person to do the same. This increases trust and strengthens your friendship.

Prioritize quality time

Spend quality time together. It may be a walk and speak in the park, a lengthy conversation over coffee, or simply sitting peacefully side by side. The goal is to be present and hold space for each other in a way that allows an emotional connection to form or deepen.

Practice appreciation

Feeling appreciated might lead to stronger sentiments of emotional connection. Acknowledge and value the little things your loved ones do for you. A simple "thank you" or "I appreciate your support" can greatly enhance your emotional link.

Seek and provide comments

A large component of emotional connection is ensuring that both parties are on the same page. It's usually a good idea to ask how the other person feels about your relationship. This might assist both of you in understanding which areas may require more effort or care. Feedback can be difficult to receive at times, so make sure you're in the appropriate frame of mind before asking for it. Try not to get defensive and maintain an open mind.

Explore mindfulness meditation
Mindfulness meditation is one of the most effective strategies to strengthen emotional connections with those you care about. Remember to calm down, concentrate on your breathing, avoid distractions, and listen. Mindfulness meditation can help you stay present during conversations with your loved ones.